Vegetarian Keto Cookbook

50 Delicious Secret Recipes to Lose Weight and Obtain A Splendid Long Lasting Physical Shape

(INCLUDING 21 days meal plan)

DR. JAMES WILLIAMS

Vegetarian Keto Cookbook

Vegetarian Keto Cookbook

Copyright ©2020 James Williams

All rights reserved.

© Copyright All rights reserved.

The transmission, duplication or reproduction of this text will be considered an illegal act regardless of whether it is carried out electronically or in print, the reproduction by third parties of the present manual (even only in part) is allowed only with an express written consent by the author. All additional rights are reserved.

Furthermore, the information on the following pages is intended solely for informational purposes and should therefore be considered universal.

The following book is reproduced below with the aim of providing information on as detailed as possible. The author cannot know the psycho-physical conditions

of every reader of this book, for this reason before undertaking one any type of action shown in the following document is always recommended the opinion of a professional who can personally verify

the conditions of the subject at 360 degrees.

There are therefore no scenarios in which the author of this work can be in any way held responsible for any issues arising incorrect use of this information or failure consulting of a professional before taking certain actions.

Vegetarian Keto Cookbook

SUMMARY

Introduction 1

CHAPTER 1 4

RECIPES FOR VEGETARIAN KETOGENIC BREAKFAST 4

Coconut donuts 5

Porridge with hemp heart.. 8

Cereals for quick breakfast 10

Pudding a thousand flavors 12

Green smoothie 14

Chocolate granola 17

Raw muesli 20

Baked omelette with asparagus and gorgonzola 22

Scrambled eggs with cheese 25

Cauliflower waffle 27

Chia pudding with blueberries 30

CHAPTER 2 32

RECIPES FOR KETOGENIC VEGETARIAN LUNCH 32

Courgette casserole... 33

Cucumber cream salad 35

Diced tomatoes and zucchini 37

Radish and zucchini quiche 39

Tagliatelle with peanut butter sauce........................... 41

Risotto with cheese 43

Cauliflower vodka casserole 46

Cauliflower and ginger stew 49

Broccoli cauliflower rice 52

Vegetable salad in a pan 54

Tomato, cucumber and olive salad 57

Mashed cabbage, cauliflower and leek........................59

Cabbage soup 61

Zucchini au gratin with cheese 64

Zucchini spaghetti with pad thai 67

Shakshuka with green eggs 71

Simple green beans 75

Guacamole stuffed eggs 77

Egg-filled peppers 80

CHAPTER 3 83

KETOGENIC VEGETARIAN 83

DINNER RECIPES 83

Tomato and basil soup 84

Cauliflower and roasted broccoli 87

Cream mushrooms soup 90

Spinach, artichoke and cauliflower casserole 93

Eggplants and eggs parmigiana 96

Tabbouleh of spinach and cucumber...........................99

Eggs with spinach and cheese 102

Mushroom risotto 105

Spaghetti with eggs and avocado 108

Nachos with Queso 111

Mediterranean zucchini spaghetti 114

Rutabaga with turnip salad 116

Cabbage salad with lime 119

Caprese with basil sauce 121

Greek cabbage wraps 124

Tofu in Shakshuka 127

Peanut tofu and cauliflower rice 130

Cauliflower in Indian masala 133

Casserole with broccoli and cheese 137

Stuffed Portobello mushrooms 140

CHAPTER 4 143

21-days meal plan 143

Conclusion 154

Introduction

Have you decided to undertake a new beneficial path to your health and yours fitness?

Have you decided to discover the potential of the ketogenic diet while respecting our own animal friends ?

Well, then you have chosen the right book ... in this volume there is everything you need to start this journey, without many rounds of words as happens in

98% of books available on the market.

This is a practical manual consisting of as many as 50 diet recipes for vegetarian ketogenic, which will help you lose weight and above all maintain a wonderful long-lasting physical form!

But what is the ketogenic diet?

The universal answer is that it's a type of power supply that foresees the increase of fats intake (in our case vegetable fats), minimizing carbohydrates intake.

Does it Sound weird? right! A diet based on the consumption of vegetable fats that it makes you lose weight...

All this is possible thanks to lipolysis and cellular lipid oxidation, in the total consumption of fats instead of carbohydrates which optimizes the slimming process.

The production of ketone bodies, which must be absolutely controlled, has also the function of moderating appetite stimulation.

This book is ideal for learning new tasty ketogenic vegetarian recipes, with a full 21-days meal plan, where they are recommended all food that you can eat during the main meals of the day!

PLEASE NOTE:

In this volume all cheese present in the recipes meant without the use of animal rennet. I usually buy this cheese listed here in large supermarkets:

Mozzarella, gorgonzola, cream cheese (example Philadelphia), Parmigiano, Feta.

Are you Ready? Let's begin!

.

CHAPTER 1
RECIPES FOR VEGETARIAN KETOGENIC BREAKFAST

Coconut donuts

Ingredients for 3 servings:

4 eggs

1/2 teaspoon baking soda

1/2 teaspoon baking powder

1/2 teaspoon coffee

1/3 cup unsweetened almond milk

1 tablespoon liquid stevia

3 tablespoons bitter cocoa powder

1/4 cup coconut oil

1/3 cup coconut flour

Instructions:

1. Preheat the oven to 180 ° C.

2. Grease a pan with oil and set it aside

3. Add all the ingredients in a large bowl and stir until they will be mixed homogeneously.

4. Pour the mixture into the pan prepared earlier and bake it for 20 minutes.

5. Decorate with coconut flakes (optional)

6. Enjoy your meal!

Nutritional values per portion:

Calories 312 kcal

Net carbs 11 g

Protein 12 g

Fat 15 g

Porridge with hemp heart

Ingredients for 1 serving:

1/4 cup almond flour

1/2 teaspoon cinnamon

3-4 teaspoons vanilla extract

5 drops liquid stevia

1 tablespoon chia seeds

2 tablespoons ground flax seeds

1/2 cup hemp seeds

1 cup unsweetened almond milk

Instructions:

1. Put all the ingredients to the saucepan and mix well
2. Put the saucepan over medium heat and cook until the contents begin to boil.
3. Mix again and cook for another 2 minutes after boiling.
4. 4.Enjoy your meal!

Nutritional values per serving:

Calories 410 kcal

Net Carbs 11 g

Protein 18 g

Fat 29 g

Cereals for quick breakfast

Ingredients for 1 serving:

1/2 tablespoon coconut flakes without sugar

1 tablespoon chia seeds

1 tablespoon ground flaxseed

2 medium strawberries

15 g pecan nuts

1/2 teaspoon vanilla

1/2 cup coconut milk

Instructions:

1. Add all the ingredients except the coconut milk in the bowl and mix well.
2. 2.Then add the coconut milk and mix again.
3. 3.Enjoy your meal!

Nutritional value :

Calories 412 kcal

Net Carbs 14 g

Protein 8 g

Fat 27 g

Pudding a thousand flavors

Ingredients for 2 servings:

2 cups coconut milk

1 cup frozen raspberries

1/4 cup MCT Oil

1 tablespoon apple cider vinegar

1 teaspoon vanilla extract

3 drops Stevia

2 tablespoons Chia Seeds

Fresh berries (optional)

Instructions:

1. Put all the ingredients in a blender.

2. Mix everything

3. Serve cold seasoned with fresh berries (optional)

4. Enjoy your meal!

Nutritional value:

Calories 388 kcal

Net Carbs 9 g

Protein 7 g

Fat 21 g

Green smoothie

Ingredients for 2 servings :

2 cups almond milk

30 g Spinach

1 Cucumber

1 Celery

1 Avocado

1 tablespoon coconut oil

10 drops liquid Stevia

1 scoop of soy Protein Powder (20g)

1/2 teaspoon Chia Seeds

Instructions:

1. Blend the spinach and almond milk together using the blender.

2. Mix the rest of the ingredients (except the chia seeds)

3. Serve by healing with chia seeds.

4. Enjoy your meal!

Nutritional values per portion:

Calories 375 kcal

Net Carbs 6 g

Protein 27 g

Fat 20 g

Chocolate granola

Ingredients for 5 servings:

50 g coconut oil

1/4 cup sweetened Cocoa

2 tablespoons granulated sweetener

1 teaspoon Cinnamon

400 g grated coconut

50 g pumpkin seeds

50 g sunflower seeds

50 g Almonds

50 g nuts

50 g flax seeds

Instructions:

1. Mix the coconut oil, cinnamon, sweetener and cocoa In powder.

2. Put all the nuts, almonds, seeds and coconut together in a baking dish .Pour with cocoa mixture created in the previous step, mix everything well.

3. Cook for 20 minutes to 180 ° C until the mixture becomes crisp and brown

4. Enjoy your meal!

Nutritional values per portion:

Calories 527 kcal

Net Carbs 9 g

Protein 26 g

Fat 39 g

Raw muesli

Ingredients for 4 servings:

2 cups grated coconut

1 cup pumpkin seeds

1 cup walnuts

1 cup sunflower seeds

1 cup sesame seeds

1 cup flaxseed

Instructions:

1. Put all the ingredients together and seal them in an airtight jar.

2. Serve by mixing them with coconut cream.

3. Enjoy your meal!

Nutritional values per portion

Calories 296 kcal

Net Carbs 8.6 g

Protein 9.4 g

Fat 26 g

Baked omelette with asparagus and gorgonzola

Ingredients for 4 servings:

220 g asparagus

3 fresh onions

2 tablespoons olive oil

6 eggs

1 cup almond milk

Salt and pepper

1/4 cup gorgonzola in pieces

Instructions:

1. Preheat the oven to 200 ° C.

2. Cut the green part of the fresh onions.

3. Cut and remove the bottom of the asparagus if it is stiff.

4. Put vegetables on a baking sheet, pour with oil and cook for 15 minutes in the oven

5. Heat the oil in a separate pan over medium heat.

6. Whisk the eggs with almond milk, salt, pepper and gorgonzola and pour this mixture in the pan (prepared in step 5) and cook for 2-3 minutes.

7. Add the asparagus and onions to the surface of the omelette (obtained in a pan) e cook for another 3 minutes.

8. Transfer the contents of the pan to the oven and continue cooking for about 10 minutes.

9. Enjoy your meal!

Nutritional values per portion:

Calories 251.7 kcal

Net Carbs 5,87 g

Protein 12.73 g

Fat 19.21 g

Scrambled eggs with cheese

Ingredients for 1 serving:

1/2 tsp salt

pinch of black pepper

1 tablespoon olive oil

1/2 cup Cream Cheese

2 eggs

Instructions:

1. Heat the butter or oil over medium heat, in the meantime break the eggs into a bowl and add salt and pepper, stirring well.

2. Cook the eggs until desired and then add the cheese Philadelphia and extend cooking by another 2 minutes.

3. Enjoy your meal!

Nutritional values per portion:

Calories 458.2 kcal

Net Carbs 2 g

Protein 25.4 g

Fat 39 g

Cauliflower waffle

Ingredients for 3 servings:

1/2 cauliflower

1 cup chopped mozzarella

1 cup green cabbage

1 egg

1/4 cup Parmesan cheese

1 tablespoon sesame seeds

2 stems green onion

2 tablespoons olive oil

2 teaspoons fresh, chopped thyme

1 teaspoon garlic powder

1/2 teaspoon ground black pepper

1 teaspoon salt

Instructions:

1. In a food processor, mince the cauliflower, spring onion, cabbage and thyme

2. Mix it with 1 cup of mozzarella, egg and 4 cups of Parmesan, 1 spoon of olive oil, 1 tablespoon of sesame seeds, 1/2 teaspoon of black pepper, 1/2 teaspoon of salt and 1 teaspoon of garlic powder in a bowl.

3. Once the mixture becomes uniform, add the mixture to the plate suitable for the waffle and cook.
4. Enjoy your meal!

Nutritional values per portion:

Calories 203 kcal

Net Carbs 5 g

Protein 14 g

Fat: 15 g

Chia pudding with blueberries

Ingredients for 2 servings:

12 tablespoons chia seeds

3 cups almond milk without sugar

1 cup water

5 drops stevia sweetener

1/4 cup blueberries

Instructions:

1. Put all the ingredients in a bowl and mix.
2. Let the mixture rest for 5 minutes and then mix again
3. Put the bowl back to the refrigerator for at least an hour.
4. Add the blueberries and serve
5. Enjoy your meal!

Nutritional values per portion:

Calories 256 kcal

Net Carbs 6 g

Protein: 10 g

Fat: 19 g

CHAPTER 2
RECIPES FOR KETOGENIC VEGETARIAN LUNCH

Courgette casserole

Ingredients for 4 servings:

4 sliced zucchini

120 g butter

1 sliced onion

1/4 cup grated Parmesan cheese

salt

pepper

Instructions:

1. In a saucepan, put the slices of zucchini, onion, butter, pepper and salt and add over the grated Parmesan
2. Cover the casserole with parchment paper and bake it to 175 ° C for 45 minutes.
3. Enjoy your meal!

Nutritional value per portion:

Calories 334 kcal

Net Carbs 9 g

Protein 12 g

Fat 23 g

Cucumber cream salad

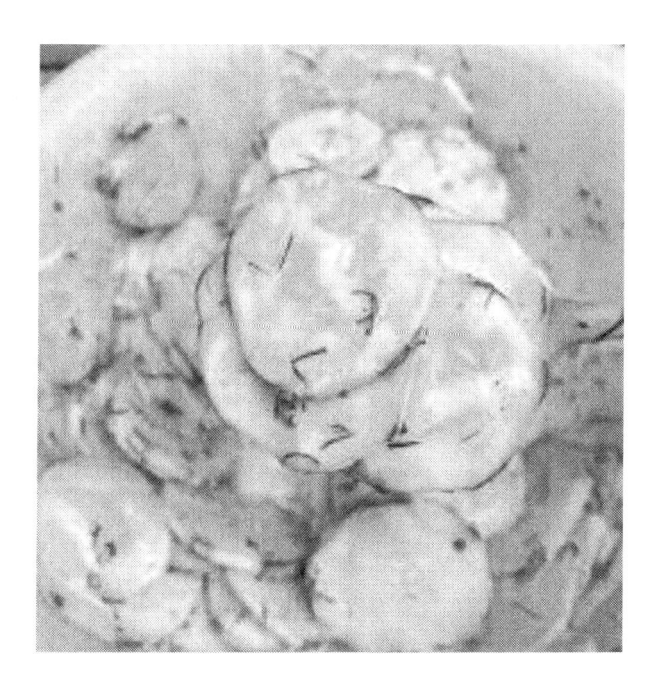

Ingredients for 2 servings:

1 sliced peeled cucumber

1 teaspoon of dill

2 teaspoons of fresh lemon juice

1 sliced onion

1 sliced tomato

1/2 cup of cream cheese

1 teaspoon salt

Instructions:

1. In a bowl, mix the cream cheese, lemon juice, dill and salt.
2. Add tomato, cucumber and onion to the bowl created in step 1 and mix well
3. Enjoy your meal!

Nutritional values per portion:

Calories 217 kcal

Net Carbs 8 g

Protein 8 g

Fat 19 g

Diced tomatoes and zucchini

Ingredients for 4 servings:

2 sliced zucchini

1 teaspoon basil

2 medium diced tomatoes

1 chopped onion

1 teaspoon butter

1/4 teaspoon pepper

1/2 teaspoon salt

Instructions :

1. Melt the butter in a pan over medium heat.
2. Add the onion and cook it until it becomes soft.
3. Add the zucchini and cook for 3 minutes.
4. Add tomatoes and basil and cook them
5. Season all with pepper and salt.
6. Enjoy your meal!

Nutritional values per portion:

Calories 93 kcal

Net Carbs 6 g

Protein 3 g

Fat 3 g

Radish and zucchini quiche

Ingredients for 4 servings:

1 zucchini blanched and sliced

2 sliced garlic cloves

8 Eggs

½ cup coconut cream

1 teaspoon salt

½ kilo radishes cut into cubes

Coconut oil for frying

Instructions:

1. Heat the coconut oil in a pan and brown the garlic and courgettes for 5 minutes.

2. Whisk the coconut cream with the eggs and a pinch of salt in a bowl.

3. Put the radish and the courgettes in a greased pan and put on the created mixture in the previous step.

4. Cook everything for 45 minutes to 160 ° C

5. Enjoy your meal!

Nutritional value per portion:

Calories 288 kcal

Net Carbs 7 g

Protein 13 g

Fat 19 g

Tagliatelle with peanut butter sauce

Ingredients for 2 servings:

2 sachets noodles kelp (seaweed)

Ingredients for sauce:

1/2 cup peanut butter

1 White onion

1/4 cup soy sauce

Juice 1 lime

2 garlic cloves

2 teaspoons chili pepper

Instructions:

1. Put all the ingredients for the sauce in a blender and blend everything well

2. Dip the noodles in water and drain.

3. Add the sauce over and enjoy your dish.

4. Enjoy your meal!

Nutritional values per portion:

Kcal: 411,

Net Carbs 9 g

Protein 16 g

Fat 29 g

Risotto with cheese

Ingredients for 4 servings:

1 Cauliflower

1/4 cup Butter

1 Chopped white onion

1 cup vegetable stock

1 teaspoon Dijon Mustard

1 cup Feta Cheese

1 cup grated Parmesan cheese

2 tablespoons Chives

Salt

Instructions:

1. Melt the butter in a pan and brown the onion lightly

2. Pour the vegetable stock and cauliflower and cook for 5 minutes.

3. Now add the mustard and stir.

4. Finally season with salt, cheese, parmesan and mix

5. Garnish with chives.

6. Enjoy your meal!

Nutritional values per portion:

Kcal: 366

Net Carbs 4 g

Protein 17 g

Fat 28 g

Cauliflower vodka casserole

Ingredients for 6 servings:

8 cups cooked cauliflower florets

2 cups vodka sauce

2 tablespoons cream cheese

2 tablespoons melted butter

1/3 cup grated Parmesan cheese

1 teaspoon salt

1/2 teaspoon black pepper

6 slices of Feta cheese

1/4 cup fresh Basil

Instructions:

1. Mix all ingredients (except basil and feta)

2. Transfer the mixture to a baking sheet and place the pieces of feta on top.

3. Bake for 30 minutes in a preheated to 190 ° C oven

4. Take it out of the oven and let it rest for 10 minutes.

5. Serve garnished with basil.

6. Enjoy your meal!

Nutritional values per portion:

Kcal: 284

Net Carbs 6 g

Protein 14 g

Fat 16 g

Cauliflower and ginger stew

Ingredients for 4 servings:

2 tablespoons coconut oil

1 Finely sliced onion

3 Chopped tomatoes

1 teaspoon cumin seeds

1 head cauliflower

1 cup cabbage

1 cup Jalapeno Seeds

2 teaspoons ginger paste

1 tablespoon cumin powder

1 teaspoon turmeric powder

1 can coconut milk

1 teaspoon salt

2 tablespoons Coriander

instructions:

1. Heat the oil in a pan and add the cumin seeds.

2. Fry the onions for a minute and then add the tomatoes.

3. Cook for a couple of minutes and then add the rest of the ingredients.

4. Cook over low heat, covering the pot for 15 minutes, stirring occasionally.

5. Enjoy your meal!

Nutritional values per portion:

Kcal: 344

Net Carbs 11 g

Protein 12 g

Fat 27 g

Broccoli cauliflower rice

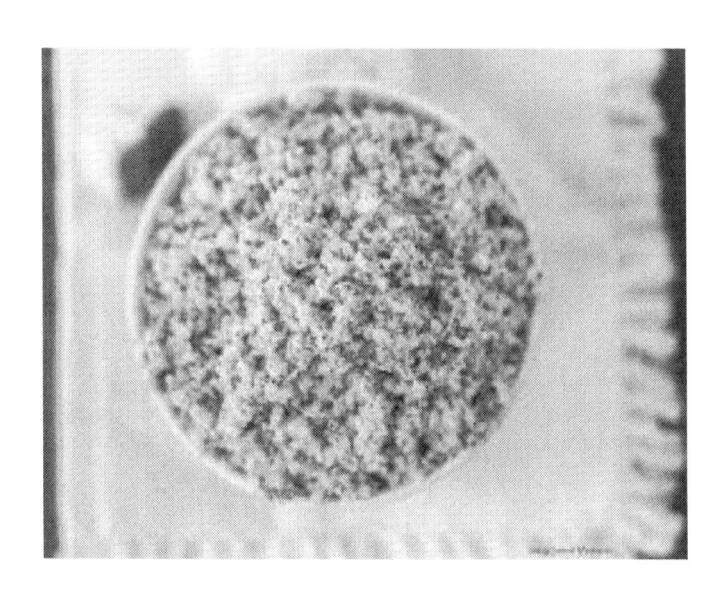

Ingredients for 3 servings:

220 g Cauliflower

100 g Broccoli

2 tablespoons water

1/4 teaspoon salt

3 tablespoons Butter

2 tablespoons Parmesan cheese

2 tablespoons lemon peel

1 clove ground garlic

90 g ground onion

Instructions:

1. Put the cauliflower, broccoli, 2 tablespoons of water together in a baking dish and cook in microwave for 2 minutes

2. Gently drain the water and mix the rest of the seasoning ingredients.

3. Enjoy your meal!

Nutritional values per portion:

Kcal: 231

Net Carbs 5 g

Protein 6 g

Fat 12 g

Vegetable salad in a pan

Ingredients for 2 servings:

2 tablespoons poppy seeds

2 tablespoons sesame seeds

1 teaspoon onion flakes

1 teaspoon garlic powder

120 g Feta cheese, sliced

1 sliced medium red pepper

1/2 cup portobello mushrooms, cut into slices

4 cups rocket sald

1 tablespoon olive oil

Instructions :

1. Combine poppy seeds, sesame seeds, onion and powdered garlic in one small bowl.
2. Dip the slices of cheese in the mixture created in step 1 and then put them in the fridge
3. Heat a pan with oil over medium heat
4. Place the pepper and mushrooms in the pan and cook them, without stirring, until they're golden brown and soften.
5. Meanwhile, place the arugula on the plate.

6. Add the pepper and mushrooms on top of the rocket salad.

7. Take the cheese from the refrigerator and lightly brown it for 30 seconds until it starts soften.

8. Add the slices of cheese to the salad and season with olive oil.

9. Enjoy your meal!

Nutritional values per portion

Kcal: 395

Net Carbs 7 g

Protein 16 g

Fat 28 g

Tomato, cucumber and olive salad

Ingredients for 1 serving:

1/4 cup olive oil Vinaigrette

1/2 chopped small onion

1/4 cup sliced olives

1/2 cup cherry tomato cut in half

1 chopped cucumber

salt

pepper

Instructions:

1. Add all the ingredients in the bowl and mix well.

2. Let the salad cool in the refrigerator for 2 hours.

3. Enjoy your meal!

Nutritional values per portion:

Kcal: 130

Net Carbs 15 g

Protein 4 g

Fat 6 g

Mashed cabbage, cauliflower and leek

Ingredients for 3 servings:

1/2 head medium cabbage

1 leek

4 cups cauliflower flowers

2 tablespoons olive oil

Chopped parsley (optional)

Salt and pepper

Instructions:

1. Wash the vegetables and chop them.

2. Heat the water in a large pot and put vegetables inside, seasoning them with salt.

3. Boil the vegetables, reducing the heat for about 20 minutes.

4. Transfer the vegetables into a blender and add the oil by blending everything.

5. Taste and season with salt and pepper.

6. Decorate with chopped parsley (optional).

7. Enjoy your meal!

Nutritional values per portion:

Kcal: 189

Net Carbs 7 g

Protein 4 g

Fat 6 g

Cabbage soup

Ingredients for 5 portions:

1 teaspoon crushed thyme

1 teaspoon salt

700 g crushed tomatoes

200 g tomato sauce

3 sliced celery stalks

3 slices of thin carrots

1 head green cabbage

1/2 head red cabbage

1 onion

4 teaspoons olive oil

Instructions:

1. Fry onion with olive oil in a large pan for five minutes.

2. separately in a saucepan, add a little water, the vegetables with tomatoes crushed, tomato sauce, beans, celery, carrots and both types of cabbage and mix well.

3. add the thyme and salt and stir.

4. Boil for 1 minute on high heat, then lower the heat and let it keep boiling for an hour.

5. Enjoy your meal!

Nutritional values per portion:

Kcal: 314

Net Carbs 14 g

Protein 15 g

Fat 13 g

Zucchini au gratin with cheese

Ingredients for 4 servings:

1/2 cup cream cheese

2 tablespoons Butter

2 cups feta cheese

1 teaspoon salt

1/2 teaspoon black pepper

1 Peeled white onion

4 cups sliced zucchini

Instructions:

1. Heat the oven to 190 ° C
2. Use some butter to grease the pan.
3. Put the onions and zucchini in the pan so that they overlap.
4. Then season with salt, pepper and 1 cup of the feta cheese.
5. Now insert another layer of onion slices and seasoned zucchini with salt and pepper and add the rest of the feta cheese.
6. Cook the cream cheese and butter, garlic powder in microwave for 1 minute until the butter melts
7. Pour the mixture on the zucchini inside the pan.

8. Bake for 45 minutes.
9. Enjoy your meal!

Nutritional values per portion:

Kcal: 230

Net Carbs 4 g

Protein 15 g

Fat 27 g

Zucchini spaghetti with pad thai

Ingredients for 3 servings:

2 tablespoons peanut oil

1 sliced onion

1 tablespoon rice vinegar

1 orange pepper

3 zucchini cut in a spiral

3 minced garlic cloves

1 tablespoon chopped fresh ginger

3 sliced shallots

2 cut carrots

2 tablespoons soy sauce

1/2 lime, squeezed

1 teaspoon chili flakes

½ cup coriander leaves

1/4 cup basil leaves

1/3 cup roasted peanuts

Instructions:

1. Pass the zucchini through the spiral cutting machine and create the noodles and then put them in a bowl.

2. Heat the zucchini noodles in the microwave for 20 seconds, eliminate water.

3. Meanwhile, heat the peanut oil and onion in the pan until they're golden brown.

4. add peppers, ginger, garlic and carrot slices. Jump for another 2 minutes.

5. Now whisk together the soy sauce, rice vinegar, chili flakes and lime juice in a bowl.

6. Add the mixture to a bowl together with the tagliatelle di zucchini and mix well.

7. Then add the shallot, the roasted peanuts, basil and coriander.

8. Mix well and serve.

9. Enjoy your meal!

Nutritional values per portion:

Kcal: 365

Net Carbs: 6 g

Protein: 6 g

Fat: 19 g

Shakshuka with green eggs

Ingredients for 4 servings:

50g spinach, chopped

8-10 fresh peeled tomatillos

4 tablespoons butter

1 cabbage cut into small pieces

1 bunch parsley

5 cloves garlic, diced

1 teaspoon salt

1 teaspoon cumin

1/2 teaspoon red pepper flakes

1/2 teaspoon of black pepper

1 lemon squeezed

1 yellow onion diced

4 eggs

4-5 sprigs dill

Instructions:

1. Preheat the oven to 180 ° C and remove the skin of the tomatillos

2. Put them in a baking dish and cook them for 8 minutes until they become soft.
3. Put them in a bowl and crush them with a fork.
4. Melt the butter over a medium heat in a large pan.
5. Stir the onions and fry them for 3 minutes
6. Add the parsley, spinach, black cabbage and toasted tomatoes.
7. Stir for 5 minutes and add the chili, cumin, juice, tomatillos and black pepper.
8. Prepare 4 small spaces in the pan and break the eggs in the center
9. Cover the pan and cook for another 5 minutes
10. Garnish with fresh dill.
11. Leave to cool a little and serve.
12. Enjoy your meal!

Nutritional values per portion:

Kcal: 371

Net Carbs 8 g

Protein 3 g

Fat 11 g

Simple green beans

Ingredients for 2 servings:

2 cups green beans

2 tablespoons butter

salt

pepper

Instructions:

1. Boil salted water over a medium heat in a saucepan.
2. Add the green beans and cook for 20 minutes, then drain
3. Add the butter to the pan and melt it over medium heat.
4. Add beans, salt and pepper.
5. Cook in a pan for 5 minutes.
4. Taste them better, serve them fresh.
5. Enjoy your meal!

Nutritional values per portion:

Kcal: 318

Net Carbs: 4 g

Protein: 4 g

Fat: 14 g

Guacamole stuffed eggs

Ingredients for 3 servings:

6 eggs

½ Hass avocado

1 teaspoon Dijon mustard

1 clove minced garlic

1 teaspoon pickle juice

1 Pinch sea salt

1 pinch black pepper

½ tsp sugar

1 tablespoon chopped fresh coriander

Instructions:

1. Put the eggs in a saucepan full of water. Boil water over medium heat.

2. Once the water boils, lower the heat and cover the casserole.

3. Let the eggs rest in boiling water for 6-12 minutes (6 minutes for the soft yolk and up to 12 minutes for a well-cooked yolk).

4. Remove the pan from the heat, drain the hot water and rinse the eggs with cold water. Peel the eggs and cut them in half. Take out the yolks and transfer them to a medium bowl. Put the egg whites aside.

5. Take the half avocado and add it to the bowl with the egg yolks.

6. Add the other ingredients (except coriander) in the bowl and crush everything together until you get a homogeneous mixture.

7. Fill each egg white with a spoonful of the mixture obtained.

8. Add a little finely chopped coriander onto it.

9. Enjoy your meal!

Nutritional values per portion:

Kcal: 270

Net Carbs: 3 g

Protein: 18 g

Fat: 25 g.

Egg-filled peppers

Ingredients for 3 servings:

6 eggs

3 peppers (red or yellow - cut in half)

2 medium Hass avocados (peeled, pitted and split into two)

1 cup tomatoes (peeled and diced)

1/4 cup chopped red onion

2 jalapenos

3 tablespoons lime juice

1 tablespoon smoked paprika powder

1 clove of garlic

1 teaspoon ground cumin seeds

1 teaspoon dried oregano

Pinch of Himalayan salt

1/4 cup of fresh chopped coriander

Instructions:

1. Preheat the oven to 190 ° C and cover a baking sheet with baking paper

2. Take a bowl, break the eggs and beat them adding salt and pepper

3. After cleaning, cut the jalapenos into small pieces.

4. Add the avocados in the bowl with the eggs, along with 2 tablespoons of lime juice, tomato, jalapenos, red onion, salt and the remaining spices (except coriander).

5. Mix everything with a potato masher or fork until

the content will be completely mixed.

6. Fill the halves of the peppers with the mixture obtained in the step previous one.

7. Transfer the 6 stuffed sweet pepper halves to the pan and cook for 30 minutes.

8. After leaving the oven, decorate the peppers with the rest of the lime juice and with coriander

9. Enjoy your meal!

Nutritional values per portion:

Kcal: 348

Net Carbs: 8 g

Protein: 16 g

Fat: 27 g

CHAPTER 3
KETOGENIC VEGETARIAN DINNER RECIPES

Tomato and basil soup

Ingredients for 1 serving:

10 diced tomatoes

2 tablespoons fresh basil

1/4 cup cream

1/4 cup vegetable broth

1 cloves garlic

1 tablespoon olive oil

1/4 teaspoon pepper

1/2 teaspoon salt

Instructions:

1. Preheat oven to 200 ° C
2. In a bowl, mix the tomatoes, olive oil and garlic and then put them in a baking dish.
3. Bake in a preheated oven for 20 minutes.
4. Transfer the cooked tomatoes to a blender and blend well.
5. Pour the tomato puree obtained in a saucepan and heat it to medium heat.
6. Add the broth and simmer for 15 minutes.

7. Add basil and cream and mix well.
8. Enjoy your meal!

Nutritional values per portion:

Kcal: 218

Net Carbs 8 g

Protein 6 g

Fat 11 g

Cauliflower and roasted broccoli

Ingredients for 5 servings:

4 cups cauliflower flowers

4 cups broccoli florets

2/3 cup grated Parmesan cheese

3 cloves garlic

1/3 cup extra virgin olive oil

salt

pepper

Instructions:

1. Preheat oven to 200 ° C.
2. In a bowl, add 1/3 cup of Parmesan, broccoli, cauliflower, garlic, oil, pepper, salt and mix well.
3. Spread the mixture on a baking sheet and bake it for 20 minutes.
4. Just before serving, add the remaining Parmesan as surface seasoning.
5. Enjoy your meal!

Nutritional values per portion:

Kcal: 216

Net Carbs: 8 g

Protein: 11 g

Fat 7 g

Cream mushrooms soup

Ingredients for 4 servings:

550 g mushrooms, cut into slices

1 cup coconut milk

1 cup cream

2 cups vegetable broth

3 cloves garlic

1/2 diced onion

1 tablespoon olive oil

A pinch pepper

1 teaspoon salt

Instructions:

1. Heat the olive oil in a large saucepan over medium heat.
2. Add mushrooms and onions to the pan and fry for 10 minutes.
3. Then add the garlic and fry for a minute.
4. Add the vegetable stock, coconut milk, cream, salt and pepper and boil.
5. Lower the heat and cook for another 15 minutes.

6. At the end of cooking, pour the mixture into a blender and whisk it up and get a creamy mix with small, pleasant pieces for the palate.
7. Enjoy your meal!

Nutritional values per portion:

Kcal: 352

Net Carbs: 9 g

Protein: 6 g

Fat: 25 g

Spinach, artichoke and cauliflower casserole

Ingredients for 4 servings:

4 cups cauliflower florets

1/4 cup Butter

1/2 cup cashew milk

225 g cream cheese rich in fat

1/2 teaspoon Kosher Salt

1/2 teaspoon black pepper

1/4 teaspoon nutmeg

1/4 teaspoon powdered garlic

1/4 teaspoon smoked Paprika

1 cup frozen spinach

3/4 cup Canned Artichokes Hearts

1 Mozzarella

1/4 cup grated Parmesan cheese

Instructions :

1. In a microwave-safe dish, mix all the ingredients (except spinach, artichoke, mozzarella and parmesan) and cook in microwave for 10 minutes.

2. Mix the rest of the ingredients separately (spinach, artichoke, mozzarella and parmesan)

leaving half a cup of mozzarella aside

3. Mix the compounds obtained in points 1 and 2 together in a saucepan and sprinkle the rest of the Parmesan on top.

4. Bake to 200 ° C for 20 minutes.

5. Add the mozzarella over the end of cooking

6. Enjoy your meal!

Nutritional values per portion:

Kcal: 422

Net Carbs: 12 g

Protein: 19 g

Fat: 31 g

Eggplants and eggs parmigiana

Ingredients for 3 servings:

700 g sliced peeled eggplants

1 cup Parmigiano

2 cups chopped mozzarella

1 cup and a half tomato sauce

Origan

Basil

1/2 teaspoon salt

Instructions:

1. Pour a little oil into a saucepan and put a row of sliced eggplants

2. Sprinkle the mozzarella into small pieces, Parmesan and the sauce

3. Repeat this process several times until the casserole is full.

4. Cover the casserole with aluminum foil and cook for 40 minutes to 190 ° C in the oven.

5. Take other pieces of mozzarella and sprinkle the top of the parmigiana, cook for another 5 minutes.

6. Enjoy your meal!

Nutritional values per portion:

Kcal: 422

Net Carbs: 15 g

Protein: 30 g

Fat: 32 g

Tabbouleh of spinach and cucumber

Ingredients for 5 servings:

3 cups cauliflower of rice

4 tablespoons extra virgin coconut oil

1 teaspoon salt

1 cucumber cut into cubes

1 cup Cherry Tomatoes

2 spring onions

3 cups Spinach

1 cup Parsley

1/2 cup mint

1/2 cup lemon juice

1 clove ground garlic

1/2 cup extra virgin olive oil

1/4 teaspoon ground black pepper

Instructions:

1. Heat the coconut oil in a pan and cook the cauliflower of rice for 5 minutes adding a pinch of salt. At the end of cooking put it aside temporarily

2. Mix olive oil, garlic and lemon juice to create a garlic sauce.
3. Add the cooked rice into cauliflower with the rest of the ingredients, including the garlic sauce prepared in step 2 and mix well.
4. Enjoy your meal!

Nutritional values per portion:

Kcal: 245

Net Carbs 10 g

Protein: 6 g

Fat: 9 g

Eggs with spinach and cheese

Ingredients for 3 servings:

6 eggs

150 g fresh spinach

170 g mozzarella cut into small pieces

1/3 cup cream cheese

1 tablespoon butter

20 g sliced green onions

1 teaspoon salt

1/2 tsp black pepper

instructions:

1. Whisk the egg, cream cheese, salt and pepper.

2. Melt the butter in a pan and brown the spinach until they are cooked

3. Put the spinach in a greased pan.

4. Sprinkle the mozzarella and green onions over it.

5. Pour the egg mixture obtained in step 1, stirring gently.

6. Cook everything in a preheated oven to 190 ° C for 35 minutes.

7. Enjoy your meal!

Nutritional values per portion:

Kcal: 339

Net Carbs: 2 g

Protein: 22 g

Fat: 24 g

Mushroom risotto

Ingredients for 4 servings:

4 and a half cups of Cauliflower

3 tablespoons coconut oil

450 g Portobello mushrooms cut into thin slices

450 g thinly sliced white mushrooms

2 pieces Shallot

1/4 cup vegetable stock

Sea salt

Ground black pepper

3 tablespoons finely chopped chives

4 tablespoons butter

1/3 cup grated Parmigiano

Instructions:

1. Heat 2 tablespoons of coconut oil in a saucepan and brown the mushrooms until when they're soften.

2. Transfer them to a bowl.

3. Put the rest of the oil in a pan and brown the shallots for 1 minute

4. Add the cauliflower and cook for 2 minutes.

5. Pour the broth and cook for another 5 minutes.

6. Remove the pan from the heat and mix with the rest of the ingredients.

7. Enjoy your meal!

Nutritional values per portion:

Kcal: 264

Net Carbs: 13 g

Protein: 11 g

Fat: 17 g

Spaghetti with eggs and avocado

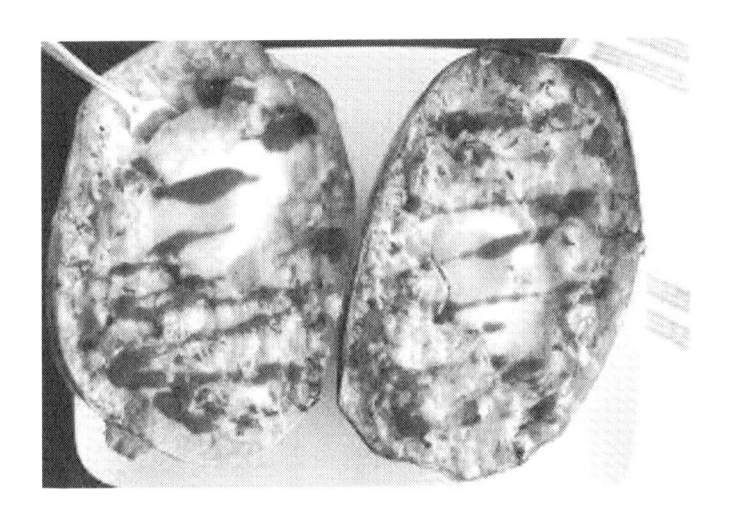

Ingredients for 2 servings:

1 zucchini to make spaghetti

1 Avocado

110 g Swiss cheese

2 eggs

2 tablespoons extra virgin olive oil

Salt and pepper to taste

2 teaspoons of Sriracha sauce

Instructions:

1. Season the zucchini with salt and pepper and add oil.

2. Cut the courgette in half and bake in a preheated oven to 200 ° C for 40 minutes.

3. cool for 15 minutes.

4. Gently scrape the pulp of the courgette, forming some "Spaghetti" and add 50 g of cheese.

5. Crush with a fork avocado and add it while stirring everything.

6. Break an egg into each half of the previously scraped courgette and insert the compound obtained in the previous step, add the remaining cheese.

7. Cook for 20 minutes to 220 ° C

8. Season with the Sriracha sauce

9. Enjoy your meal!

Nutritional values per portion:

Kcal: 559

Net Carbs: 16 g

Protein: 22 g

Fat: 33 g

Nachos with Queso

Ingredients for 2 servings:

For tortilla chips:

60 g ground flax seeds

1/2 teaspoon salt

1/2 cup water

For the Queso:

1 cup peeled hemp seeds

1 cup water

2 tablespoons food yeast

½ teaspoon cayenne powder

½ teaspoon garlic powder

½ tsp onion powder

½ tsp paprika

3 tablespoons MTC oil

½ salt

Nacho condiments:

2 servings Beyond Meat Feisty Crumbles (fake meat)

30 g cut black olives

2 tablespoons sauce (your choice)

1 tablespoon sliced green onions

Instructions:

1. Mix the ingredients of tortilla well in a bowl and set them aside for some minutes.

2. Distribute the mixture in a thin layer on a baking sheet lined with parchment

paper and Bake to 180 degrees for 30 minutes

3. heat the Beyond Meat Feisty Crumbles and set it aside.

4. Separately, blend all the ingredients to prepare the queso, until you reach one homogeneous consistency.

5. Once the mixture of point 2 is ready, add the feisty beyond meat heated crumbles, olives, sauce, green onions and 1/4 cup queso

6. Enjoy your meal!

Nutritional values per portion:

Kcal: 385

Net Carbs: 15 g

Protein: 23 g

Fat: 29 g

Mediterranean zucchini spaghetti

Ingredients for 1 serving:

1 pack shirataki noodles

1/2 cup lupine beans

1 cup spinach

30 g sliced black olives

2 pieces dried tomatoes

1 clove minced garlic

3 tablespoons olive oil

Salt and pepper

Instructions:

1. Cook the lupine beans, tomatoes, minced garlic, olives and spinach together in a covered pan with olive oil over medium-low heat until the spinach is cooked

2. Mix shirataki noodles with the compound from the previous step.

3. Cook in the closed pan until excess liquid is eliminated.

4. Add salt and pepper and serve.

5. Enjoy your meal!

Nutritional values per portion:

Calories: 387 kcal

Carbs: 15 g

Protein: 17 g

Fat 16 g

Rutabaga with turnip salad

Ingredients for 4 servings:

450g small rutabaga

2 turnips

1 tablespoon lemon juice

1/2 teaspoon Dijon mustard

Kosher salt

2 finely chopped onions

3 tablespoons extra virgin olive oil

1 tablespoon fresh parsley, finely chopped

Instructions:

1. Cut the ends of the root and stem of the rutabaga, peel it and cut it to long.

2. Cut and peel the turnips with a potato peeler.

3. In a medium bowl, mix together the lemon juice, mustard and salt.

4. Add the rutabaga to the bowl of step 3 and let it rest for 15 minutes.

5. Add the turnip and spring onions (only the white parts), and leave to rest for 5 more minutes.

6. Pour the olive oil, parsley and the green parts of the shallots and mix well.

7. Enjoy your meal!

Nutritional values per portion:

Calories 198 kcal

Net Carbs 7 g

Protein 3 g

Fat 4 g

Cabbage salad with lime

Ingredients for 4 servings:

1 teaspoon salt

1/4 cup water

1 clove garlic

2 tablespoons lime juice

1/4 cup fresh coriander leaves

2 avocados

400 g ready-made cabbage salad

Instructions:

1. Chop coriander and garlic and put them in a blender with a little bit of water, add 2 avocados, lime juice and blend.

2. Mix the cabbage salad mix with the sauce you've just got and mix good

3. Enjoy your meal!

Nutritional values per portion:

Calories 359 kcal

Carbs 5 g

Protein 8 g

Fat 12 g

Caprese with basil sauce

Ingredients for 3 servings:

Condiments

1 teaspoon salt

2 tablespoons olive oil

2 tablespoons lemon juice

1 tablespoon powdered garlic

1 teaspoon Basil

Tomato Dressing:

1 tablespoon Basil

16 thin slices Mozzarella

½ tsp black pepper

2 tablespoons balsamic vinegar

1 tablespoon olive oil

8 Tomatoes

Instructions:

1. Preheat oven to 170 ° C.
2. Cut tomatoes in half and place them on the baking tray
3. Grease each half of the tomato with a mixture of balsamic vinegar, olive oil,

lemon juice, garlic powder, chopped salt basil and black pepper.

4. Bake in the oven for 25 minutes.
5. Place one of the thin slices of mozzarella on each half of the tomato and cook them for another 5 minutes. Put chopped basil on each tomato for embellishment
6. Enjoy your meal!

Nutritional values per portion:

Calories 240 kcal

Carbs 4 g

Protein 6 g

Fat 9 g

Greek cabbage wraps

Ingredients for 4 servings:

Seasoning:

1/2 cup olive oil

2 tablespoons red wine vinegar

½ tsp black pepper

½ tsp salt

1/4 tsp oregano

1 clove of garlic

Salad preparation:

½ tsp salt

1 cup Feta cheese

½ cup sliced black olives

½ cup Parsley

1 red onion

1 peeled cucumber

1 cup cherry tomatoes

1 Yellow pepper cut into cubes

4 cups Romaine lettuce

2 tablespoons of olive oil

Instructions:

1. Mix all the seasoning ingredients listed in a bowl and put them aside for a few minutes.
2. Use another larger bowl to mix all the salad ingredients.
3. Now mix the 2 compounds previously obtained in a larger bowl.
4. Finally, cut it over the feta cheese.
5. Enjoy your meal!

Nutritional values per serving:

Calories 294 kcal

Net Carb 11 g

Protein 15 g

Fat 15 g

Tofu in Shakshuka

Ingredients for 3 servings:

1 tablespoon olive oil

2 cloves garlic

150g diced tomatoes

Salt and pepper

1/2 tsp dried chilli flakes

1 teaspoon stevia sweetener

1 medium block of tofu cut into small pieces

Indian black salt

Instructions:

1. Heat the cooking oil in a pan and fry the garlic over medium heat.
2. Add salt, pepper, chili pepper, sweetener and tomatoes.
3. Cook for 5 minutes.
4. Add the tofu and continue cooking for another 15 minutes.
5. Add black salt for seasoning.
6. Enjoy your meal

Nutritional values per portion:

Calories 291 kcal

Carbs 7 g

Protein 13 g

Fat: 11 g

Peanut tofu and cauliflower rice

Ingredients for 3 servings:

Ingredients for sautéed Tofu:

340 g extra hard tofu

1 tablespoon toasted sesame oil

1 cauliflower with small head

2 minced garlic cloves

Ingredients for SALSA:

2 tablespoons sesame oil

1/4 cup low sodium soy sauce

½ tsp chili and garlic sauce

2 tablespoons peanut butter

Instructions:

1. Drain and then squeeze the tofu to remove all the excess water.
2. Preheat the oven to 200 ° C and in the meantime cut the tofu into cubes.
3. Put the parchment paper in the pan.
4. Now put the tofu cubes in the pan and cook them for 25 minutes
5. Mix all other ingredients of the sauce in a separate bowl and pour over the tofu.

6. After that, let it rest for 15 minutes.
7. Fry the garlic with the cauliflower using sesame oil in a pan for 8 minutes.
8. Mix the cauliflower with the tofu.
9. Enjoy your meal!

Nutritional values per portion:

Calories 415 kcal

Carbs 8 g

Protein 6 g

Fat 28 g

Cauliflower in Indian masala

Ingredients for 3 servings:

2 diced onions

5 diced tomatoes

1 cauliflower head

½ cup cashews

1 teaspoon chopped ginger

1 teaspoon minced garlic

2 tablespoons oil

1 bay leaf

½ tsp cumin seeds

1/4 teaspoon pepper

1 green cardamom

3 cloves

2 black cardamoms

½ tsp garam masala

1 tablespoon coriander, chopped

1/2tsp turmeric powder

1 teaspoon coriander powder

1 teaspoon toasted sesame seeds (optional)

Salt

2 cups water

Instructions:

1. Preheat the pot with oil.

2. Add the cumin seeds, black cardamom, bay leaf, green cardamom, black pepper and cloves.

3. Brown for 30 seconds and then add the onions, garlic and ginger.

4. Stir for 5 minutes and add the spices.

5. Cook for 2 minutes and add the tomatoes, stirring.

6. Add the cashews

7. Now Blend the mixture using a blender

8. Put everything in a saucepan and slowly add some hot water continuously the mixture.

9. Add the cauliflower to the mixture and put the lid on the pan

10. Then cook over medium heat for 10 minutes

11. Garnish with sesame seeds, garam masala, and coriander.

12. Enjoy your meal!

Nutritional values per portion:

Calories 467 kcal

Carbs 9 g

Protein 6 g

Fat 25 g

Casserole with broccoli and cheese

Ingredients for 3 servings:

3 cups diced broccoli florets

2 tablespoons hot water

1 cup cream cheese

1 cup Feta cheese into small pieces

1/4 cup wholegrain mayonnaise

1 tablespoon avocado oil

1 teaspoon garlic powder

½ tsp ground black pepper

1 pinch of salt

Instructions:

1. Preheat the oven to 175 ° C.
2. In a saucepan, add the diced broccoli and water.
3. Add the cheese, mayonnaise, avocado oil and spices and mix well.
4. Complete the dish with a little bit of extra ground black pepper and salt.
5. Transfer the casserole into the oven and cook for 10 minutes.

6. Enjoy your meal!

Nutritional values per portion:

Calories 633 kcal

Carbs 6 g

Protein 24 g

Fat 58 g

Stuffed Portobello mushrooms

Ingredients for 2 servings:

4 Portobello mushrooms (without stem)

4 tablespoons butter

1 cup frozen spinach (thawed and drained)

1 cup artichoke hearts (drained and chopped)

½ cup grated Parmesan

1/4 cup cream cheese

½ cup mozzarella

½ tsp garlic powder

Salt and pepper

Instructions:

1. Preheat the oven to 190 ° C and cover the pan with aluminum paper.

2. After cleaning the mushrooms, cover each "cap" of the mushrooms with the butter.

3. Place the mushroom caps on the pan, bake for 5 minutes and then turn them over and cook them for another 5 minutes.

4. Meanwhile, remove excess water left in the spinach using a sieve.

5. In a bowl, mix the spinach, the artichoke, the Parmesan, the cream of cheese, garlic powder,

salt and pepper.

6. Fill each mushroom stopper with this mixture.

7. Finally, add the mozzarella and cook the mushrooms for another 10 minutes.

8. Enjoy your meal!

Nutritional values per portion:

Calories 479 kcal

Carbs 6 g

Protein 23 g

Fat 38,5 g

CHAPTER 4
21-days meal plan

Day 1

Breakfast:

Coconut donuts

Lunch:

Courgette casserole

Dinner:

Tomato and basil soup

Day 2

Breakfast:

Porridge with hemp heart

Lunch:

Cream cucumber salad

Dinner:

Cauliflower and roasted broccoli

Day 3

Breakfast:

Cereals for a quick breakfast

Lunch:

Diced tomatoes and zucchini

Dinner:

Cream mushrooms soup

Day 4

Breakfast:

Pudding

Lunch:

Radish and zucchini quiche

Dinner:

Casserole of spinach, artichokes and cauliflower

Day 5

Breakfast:

Green smoothie

Lunch:

Tagliatelle with peanut butter sauce

Dinner:

Eggs and eggplants parmigiana

Day 6

Breakfast:

Chocolate Granola

Lunch:

Cheese risotto

Dinner:

Tabbouleh of spinach and cucumber

Day 7

Breakfast:

Raw muesli

Lunch:

Cauliflower vodka casserole

Dinner:

Eggs with spinach and cheese

Day 8

Breakfast:

Baked omelette with asparagus and gorgonzola

Lunch:

Stew of cauliflower and ginger

Dinner:

Mushrooms Risotto

Day 9

Breakfast:

Scrambled eggs with cheese

Lunch:

Rice with broccoli and cauliflower

Dinner:

Spaghetti with eggs and avocado

Day 10

Breakfast:

cauliflower waffle

Lunch:

Vegetable salad in a pan

Dinner:

Nachos con queso

Day 11

Breakfast:

Chia pudding with blueberries

Lunch:

Salad with tomatoes, cucumbers and olives

Dinner:

Mediterranean zucchini spaghetti

Day 12

Breakfast:

Coconut donuts

Lunch:

Mashed cabbage, cauliflower and leek

Dinner:

Rutabaga with turnip salad

Day 13

Breakfast:

Porridge with hemp heart

Lunch:

Cabbage soup

Dinner:

Lime cabbage salad

Day 14

Breakfast:

Cereals for a quick breakfast

Lunch:

Zucchini au gratin with cheese

Dinner:

Caprese with basil sauce

Day 15

Breakfast:

Pudding

Lunch:

Zucchini spaghetti with pad thai

Dinner:

Greek cabbage wraps

Day 16

Breakfast:

Green smoothie

Lunch:

Shakshuka with green eggs

Dinner:

Tofu in Shakshuka

Day 17

Breakfast:

Chocolate granola

Lunch:

Simple green beans

Dinner:

Peanut tofu and cauliflower rice

Day 18

Breakfast:

Raw muesli

Lunch:

Eggs filled with guacamole

Dinner:

Cauliflower in Indian masala

Day 19

Breakfast:

Baked omelette with asparagus and gorgonzola

Lunch:

Egg-filled peppers

Dinner:

Casserole with broccoli and cheese

Day 20

Breakfast:

Scrambled eggs with cheese

Lunch:

Stew of cauliflower and ginger

Dinner:

Stuffed portobello mushrooms

Day 21

Breakfast:

Chia pudding with blueberries

Lunch:

Courgette casserole

Dinner:

Mushrooms Risotto

Conclusion.

Thank you so much for reading this book, but first of all accept my congratulations for choosing to discover these 50 delicious and healthy ketogenic recipes.

Meat was at the center of the ketogenic diet until a few years ago, now it is not anymore so ...

In fact, even in nature you can easily find sources of fat and protein perfectly suited to start a process of ketosis in our body.

You will certainly have noticed the vastness of the ketogenic recipes that you can have fun to create without being a chef ...

All ingredients of the recipes given in this manual are easy available in supermarkets or in some cases even on the internet!

You will be able to have fun creating delicious smoothies for breakfast, delicious omelettes and

many other dishes that you surely didn't know before the consultation of this volume!

Is It seem hard to imagine a food plan without carbohydrates? Is it right?

And instead, it was easier than expected because you can live in great shape simply by increasing the fat load and reducing that of carbohydrates.

PS: Ah ... I only forgot one last thing, very important for me ... if you liked it, I kindly ask you to leave a 5-star review.

I know, for you it means losing a minute of your time, but for me it would mean a lot and your review would be a great help for all the work I have done.

I wish you a good life!